EVERYTHING SPORTS

EVERYTHING SOFTBALL

SEAN SHAPIRO

An Imprint of Abdo Publishing
abdobooks.com

abdobooks.com

Published by Abdo Publishing, a division of ABDO, PO Box 398166, Minneapolis, Minnesota 55439.

Printed in China.
052024
092024

Cover Photos: Nate Billings/AP Images (Tiare Jennings); Tyler Schank/NCAA Photos/Getty Images (Devyn Flaherty); iStockphoto (background)
Interior Photos: Ian Maule/Getty Images Sport/Getty Images, 4–5; Justin Tafoya/NCAA Photos/Getty Images, 7; Oscar White/VCG/Corbis Historical/Getty Images, 8–9; Los Angeles Examiner/USC Libraries/Corbis Historical/Getty Images, 11; Luis Gutiérrez/Norte Photo/Getty Images Sport/Getty Images, 12–13; Thurman James/Cal Sport Media/AP Images, 15; Brian Bahr/Getty Images Sport/Getty Images, 16, 32–33, 44–45, 47; Yuichi Masuda/Getty Images Sport/Getty Images, 18–19, 26–27; Tommy Martino/University of Montana/Getty Images Sport/Getty Images, 20–21; Jacob Snow/Icon Sportswire/Getty Images, 23; Kevin Sullivan/Digital First Media/Orange County Register/MediaNews Group/Getty Images, 24–25; Elise Amendola/AP Images, 28; Daisuke Tomita/Yomiuri Shimbun/AP Images, 30–31; Chris Landsberger/NCAA Photos/Getty Images, 34; Stephen Pingry/NCAA Photos/Getty Images, 36–37, 42–43; Shane Bevel/NCAA Photos/Getty Images, 38–39; Tony Duffy/Getty Images Sport/Getty Images, 41; Colin E. Braley/AP Images, 48–49; Zac BonDurant/Icon Sportswire/Getty Images, 51; Lachlan Cunningham/AP Images, 52–53; Quinn Harris/Getty Images Sport/Getty Images, 54–55; Joel Lerner/Xinhua News Agency/Getty Images, 56; Joel Robine/AFP/Getty Images, 59; Shizuo Kambayashi/AP Images, 61

Editor: Charlie Beattie
Series Designer: Karli Kruse

Library of Congress Control Number: 2023949396
Publisher's Cataloging-in-Publication Data
Names: Shapiro, Sean, author.
Title: Everything softball / by Sean Shapiro
Description: Minneapolis, Minnesota: Abdo Publishing, 2025 | Series: Everything sports | Includes online resources and index.
Identifiers: ISBN 9781098293611 (lib. bdg.) | ISBN 9798384912880 (ebook)
Subjects: LCSH: Softball--Juvenile literature. | Fastpitch softball--Juvenile literature. | Softball players--Juvenile literature. | Softball teams--Juvenile literature. | Pitching (Softball)--Juvenile literature. | Softball injuries--Juvenile literature. | Softball--Records--Juvenile literature. | Softball--Rules--Juvenile literature. | Sports--Juvenile literature.
Classification: DDC 796.3578--dc23

CHAPTER ONE

WHAT IS SOFTBALL?

The batter digs in. The pitcher stares in at the catcher's signals. She shakes her head. Finally, they decide on which pitch they want thrown. The pitcher goes into her windmill windup and fires. The batter swings through the rising fastball, which makes a loud "pop" as it hits the catcher's mitt.

Softball has its roots in baseball. But over the years, it has developed into its own game. Its history, rules, and variations make it popular with players and fans worldwide.

Softball involves two teams competing to score the most runs. Games are typically divided into seven innings. Each team has an opportunity to bat and play in the field in every inning. The playing field, referred to as a diamond, features bases, an infield, an outfield, and a pitcher's circle.

University of Oklahoma pitcher Alex Storako shows emotion after a strikeout during the 2023 Women's College World Series (WCWS).

SLOW-PITCH SOFTBALL

There are two different versions of softball. Fast-pitch is played competitively at the highest levels of sport. Slow-pitch is most often viewed as a recreational game, though some leagues and tournaments use this version of the game. Both types of softball are played on the same fields. The pitchers throw underhand in both games. But in slow-pitch, the ball is pitched in a high arc that's easier to hit. That makes the game more accessible for people of all ages and abilities.

A softball is larger and heavier than a baseball. Players use other specialized equipment, including bats and gloves. On offense, players use bats to hit a ball when it's pitched to them. Defensive players wear thick, padded gloves to catch and field the ball.

Innings follow a simple structure. The team up to bat sends a batter to home plate. The opposing team's pitcher delivers the ball. The pitcher's goal is to strike out the batter or get an out via a batted ball. The batter tries to hit the ball in fair territory and then run around the bases. If a batter/runner makes it all the way home before the defense records three outs, it counts as a run. Whichever team has more runs after seven innings wins.

Though softball has been played for more than a century, it's still gaining a foothold on the sports world's biggest stages. Women's softball debuted as an Olympic sport in 1996. But it's been in and out of the Games since then.

The 2023 WCWS attracted a record average of 12,257 fans per game.

College and international women's softball leagues have surged in popularity. Men's fast-pitch softball is less popular but has a strong following where it is played.

CHAPTER TWO

THE FIRST GAME

Softball is most closely related to baseball, which first gained popularity in the United States in the mid-1800s. But softball owes its existence to a different sport—college football. On Thanksgiving Day 1887, the football teams of Harvard and Yale renewed their budding rivalry. Meanwhile, a group of men gathered at the Farragut Boat Club in Chicago. When they found out Yale had won the game, one man celebrated by throwing an old boxing glove toward another fan. The second fan was holding a broomstick, and he swung it at the boxing glove.

Reporter George Hancock watched the scene unfold. It gave him an idea. He suggested the men divide into teams and play a game of "indoor baseball." They used the boxing glove as a ball and the broomstick as a bat. A piece of

The famous Harvard-Yale football game had a hand in the invention of softball.

chalk came in handy for drawing the baselines, bases, and pitcher's mound.

RUN WHICH WAY?

One of the variations of early indoor baseball came from Albert Spalding. He was a former baseball player and owned a sporting goods company. Spalding's version of the game had a unique twist: the first batter of the inning could decide which direction to run around the bases, clockwise or counterclockwise. The rest of the batters that inning had to follow suit.

The final score of the first game was 41–40. Hancock was happy with his experiment. He spent the winter writing rules of his new sport. The next spring, Hancock brought the game outside. He called it Indoor-Outdoor and played it on a smaller version of a baseball field. The first official rule book was adopted in 1889.

The sport quickly gained popularity within Chicago and soon expanded beyond the city's limits. The modified rules, softer ball, and smaller playing field made it easier to play. That attracted a wider range of players, both men and women, young and old.

As the years passed, different regions and communities added their unique twists to the game. In the 1890s, Lewis Rober, a fire department officer from Minneapolis,

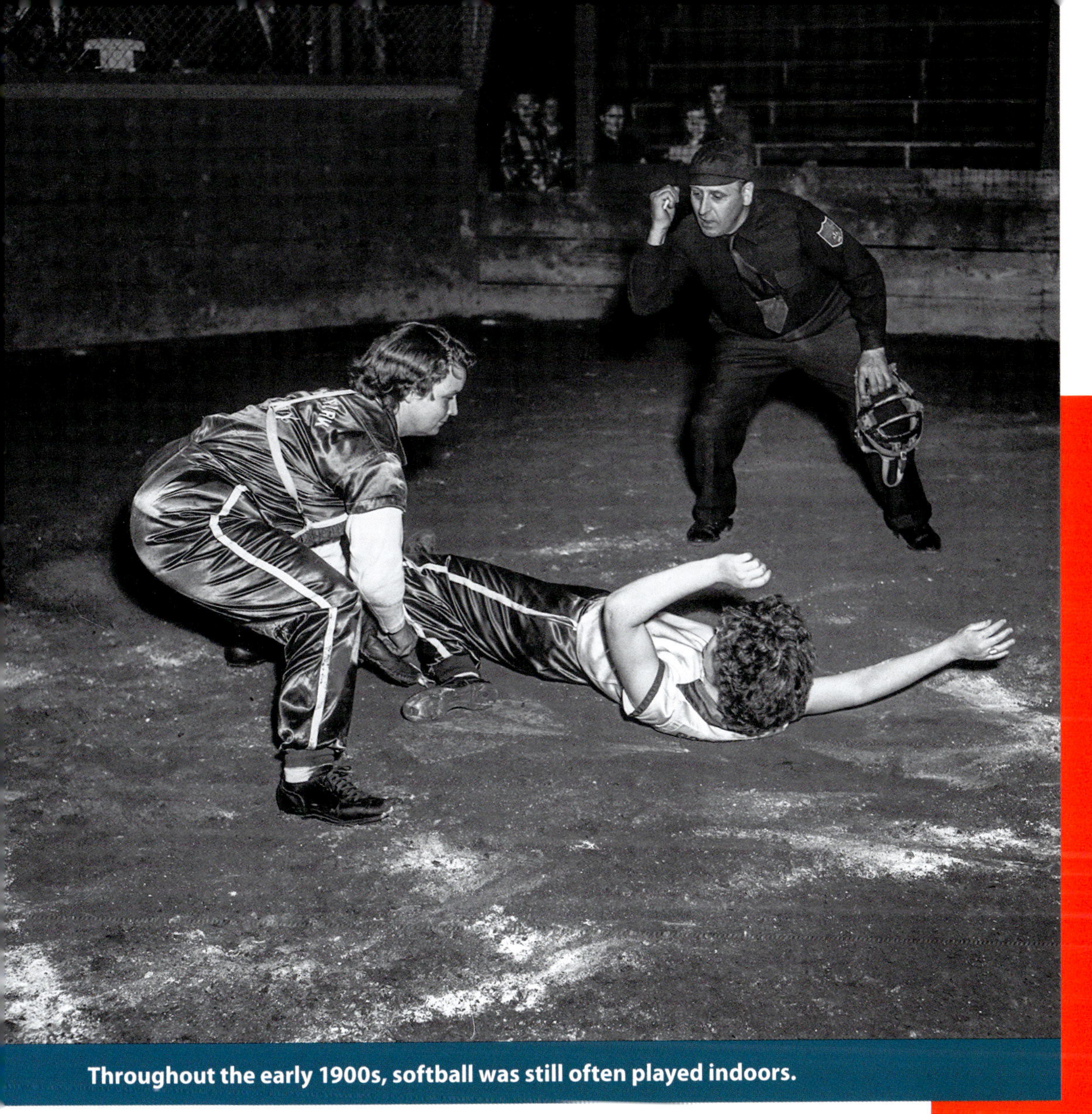

Throughout the early 1900s, softball was still often played indoors.

Minnesota, wanted his crew to get some exercise between alarms. When he realized that hitting the ball looked a little bit like a cat hitting a ball of string, Rober named his team the Kittens. Because of the name, members of his fire crew started calling the game they were playing "kitten ball."

As the sport evolved, the name softball eventually caught on. It was credited to Walter Hakanson, an educator from Denver. He coined the term in the mid-1920s, and by 1930 it was widely used across the country.

A big tournament was staged at the 1933 World's Fair in Chicago. Fifty-five teams took part. That event led to the founding of the Amateur Softball Association (ASA), which helped set the agreed upon rules of the game. Today, softball is played in many ways and at many different levels. They range from recreational leagues to competitive international tournaments. They all got their start with a broom and a boxing glove, and grew from there thanks to Hancock, Rober, and Hakanson.

Though mostly played by women, there are men's softball leagues and competitions around the world.

CHAPTER THREE

UNDERHAND PITCHING

When George Hancock adapted baseball to be played indoors, he made many important changes. One of the most important differences is the way the ball is pitched. Due to the smaller field size, the pitcher had to stand closer to home plate. To give the batters a better chance of hitting the ball, he decided to have pitchers throw underhand. At the time, many baseball pitchers threw sidearm. So the idea of underhand pitching wasn't that different of an idea.

Over time, this underhand pitching style became an important part of softball's identity. Underhand pitching puts less stress on the shoulder and arm, so pitchers are less likely to get injured. That makes it easier for young players to try pitching. And it gives young pitchers a chance to work on their skills with a limited risk of injury.

The process of fast-pitch softball pitching requires precision, skill, and practice. There are a few key components of the underhand pitch. The first is the grip. The pitcher typically holds the ball with the fingertips, using a grip that offers control and spin. What grip a pitcher uses depends on the type of pitch they want to throw.

Softball pitches must be released from below the pitcher's hip.

The pitcher starts with their front foot on the rubber—a white slab located 40 to 43 feet (12–13 m) from home plate. The windup phase involves a step back and a circular motion with the arm to generate power. As the pitcher steps forward

Pitchers can adjust the spin and speed of the ball by changing their grip.

with their glove-side foot, they bring their throwing arm forward. They release the ball from below their waistline with their hand sweeping forward and upward. Like the different grips, where the ball is released often depends on which pitch is being thrown.

Finally, a pitcher must follow through. After releasing the ball, the pitcher follows through with their throwing arm, bringing it across their body. This motion helps with accuracy and balance.

Softball pitchers use a variety of pitches. Common pitches include the fastball, changeup, curveball, rise, and drop. Each relies on different wrist and arm movements to make the ball spin properly.

While underhand pitches aren't thrown as fast as overhand pitches, they are challenging to hit. The underhand motion gives a pitcher greater control. That makes it possible to hit spots in the strike zone consistently. It also lets pitchers use a wide array of spin and movement on the ball to deceive batters. In addition, softball pitchers

THE FASTEST PITCH

American Monica Abbott threw the fastest pitch in competition, according to Guinness World Records. In a June 2012 National Pro Fastpitch (NPF) game, one of Abbott's pitches was clocked at 77 mph (123.9 km/h).

are 43 feet (13 m) away from home plate at the professional level. That is roughly 17 feet (5 m) closer to home than baseball pitchers. Because of that difference, a softball pitch traveling 60 miles per hour (97 km/h) is similar to a baseball pitch traveling 95 miles per hour (153 km/h). In both cases, the hitter has about 1/2 of a second to react.

Batters also have to hit a ball that can change direction mid-flight due to spin and air resistance. The underhand style demands quick reflexes from batters. The art of underhand pitching in softball has changed a lot over the years. Pitchers have developed new grips, variations, and tactics to keep batters guessing.

Legendary pitcher Cat Osterman was known to have pinpoint control despite throwing roughly 60 to 65 miles per hour (97–105 km/h).

CHAPTER FOUR

TOOLS OF THE TRADE

Like all sports, softball has a list of basic equipment needed to play the game. It starts with the ball. Softballs come in various sizes and can be made of different materials. The ball used in fast-pitch is 11 inches (28 cm) around. That's two inches bigger than a baseball. Slow-pitch teams generally use a 12-inch (30-cm) ball. Despite the name of the game, softballs are not actually soft. They are wrapped in leather or synthetic material that makes the outside tough and very hard.

Softball bats are specifically designed for the sport. They come in various lengths and weights to suit different player preferences. They cannot be bigger than 34 inches (86 cm) long or 2 1/4 inches (6 cm) in diameter. They also cannot weigh more than 31 1/2 ounces (0.9 kg). Bats can be made

College softball has used yellow balls since 1993. The brighter balls are easier to see.

CHICAGO BALL

In Chicago, people play a version of slow-pitch named after the city. The ball used in Chicago Ball is 16 inches (41 cm) around. It's also softer, which limits how hard the ball can be hit. Because of the softer ball, players in Chicago Ball don't wear gloves.

from a variety of materials. Many modern softball bats are made from aluminum alloy, known for both its durability and consistency.

Composite softball bats are made from high-tech materials such as carbon fiber. The area of the bat that players usually want to meet the ball is called the sweet spot. The sweet spot on composite bats is usually larger than those made from aluminum alloy. Meanwhile, some softball bats are made from both aluminum alloy and composite materials. These hybrid bats aim to offer the best of both worlds. They bring the durability of an alloy and the performance benefits of composite.

Fielders' gloves are designed to help players catch and control the ball. They also provide protection. They are bigger than baseball gloves. They also have a deeper pocket to handle the larger ball. Softball gloves come in various sizes. Which glove a player uses often depends on their position. Infielders typically use smaller gloves. They make it easier to quickly transfer the ball to the bare hand for a throw. Outfielders use larger gloves to pull in more fly balls.

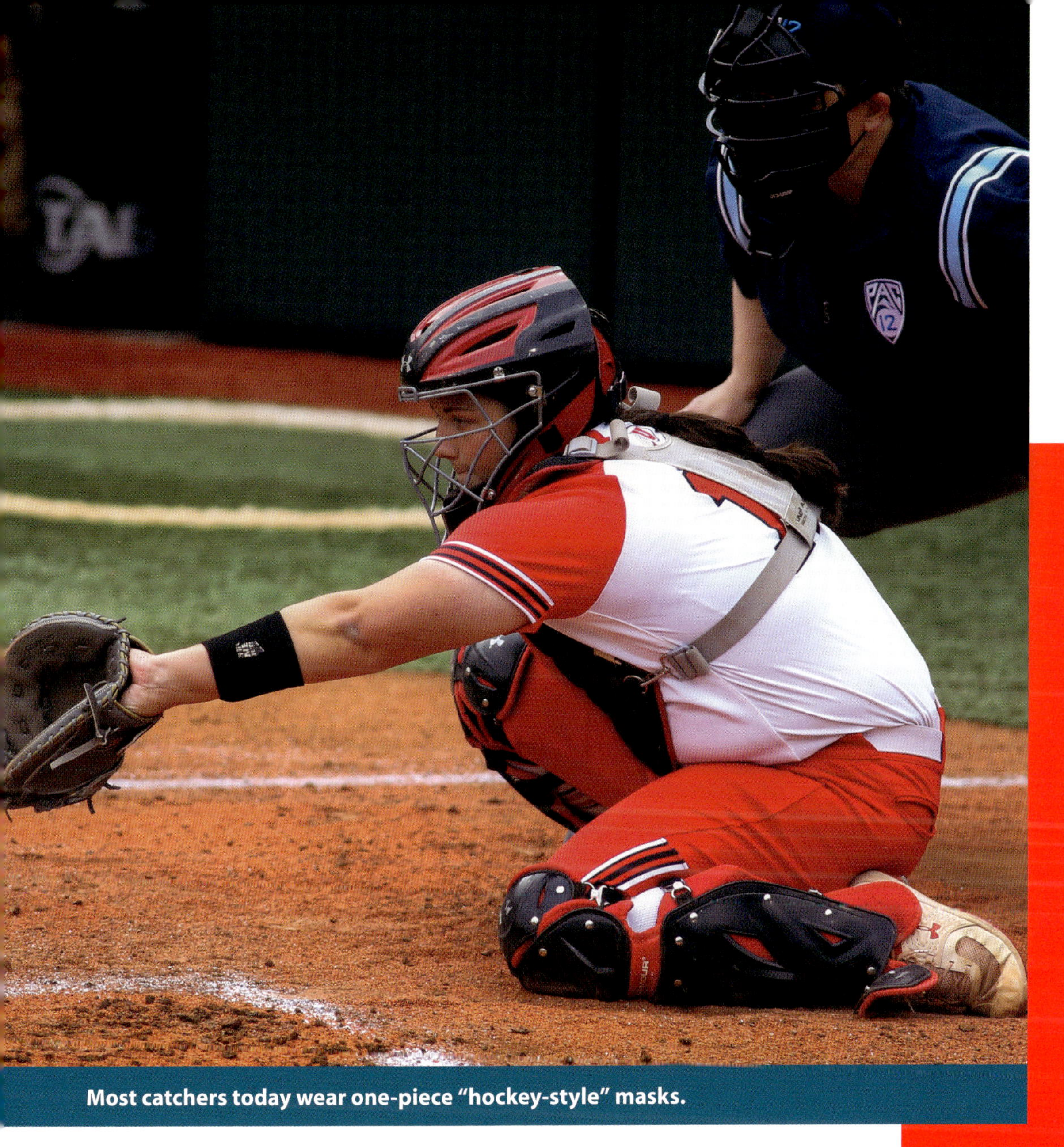
Most catchers today wear one-piece "hockey-style" masks.

Since catcher is an especially dangerous position, it comes with a special set of safety gear. This equipment typically includes a chest protector, shin guards, a helmet and mask with a throat guard, and a catcher's mitt. The gear protects the catcher from foul tips, wild pitches, and potential collisions at the plate. The mitt has extra padding so the hand won't get sore from catching too many fastballs.

Batting helmets are important for player protection. These helmets feature a hard outer shell and cushioning on the inside to absorb impact. They also include a faceguard to shield the batter's face from wild pitches. Younger players may also be required to wear protective facemasks in addition to the helmet.

Some players wear protective masks or faceguards while in the field. Pitchers, first basemen, and third basemen have the greatest need for protection. That's because they start every play closer to home plate than their teammates. That puts them at a higher risk of being hit in the face by a batted ball.

In 2006, a national rule was adopted requiring high school batters to wear facemasks.

CHAPTER FIVE

OLYMPIC SOFTBALL

Softball has had a bit of a roller-coaster experience in the Olympics. The Games have featured many thrilling softball moments. But the Olympics have also snubbed the sport, casting doubt on its future as a full-time core Olympic event.

The movement to make softball an Olympic sport goes back to the 1960s. The head of the International Softball Federation first pitched the idea to the International Olympic Committee (IOC) in 1965. At the time, he was told the sport wasn't played in enough countries to make it a good fit for the Olympics. It took years of patience and persistence. But finally, in 1991, the IOC voted to include softball as a medal sport for the 1996 Games in Atlanta, Georgia.

Team USA left fielder Janie Reed makes a leaping catch at the fence during the Olympic Games in Yokohama, Japan, in 2021.

The United States takes a lap around the field after winning the gold medal at the 1996 Olympics.

The first Olympic softball tournament was a hit, especially in the United States. The US team took gold, and played to huge crowds along the way. More than 120,000 fans attended softball games in Georgia. American women were successful in several sports at the 1996 Games. Team USA also took home gold in women's basketball, soccer, and gymnastics. But it was the popularity of softball that proved to be the biggest surprise of all.

PERFECTION

Team USA's domination was the main story of the 2004 Olympic softball tournament. But Japan pitcher Yukiko Ueno made history, too. She threw a seven-inning perfect game against China, retiring all 21 batters she faced. That made her the first—and to date, only—pitcher with a seven-inning perfect game in Olympic competition.

"We kept getting bigger attendances with each game," US shortstop Dot Richardson said. "Then, for the gold-medal game, I heard [people were making money by reselling their] tickets. For softball! Can you imagine that?"

Olympic exposure gave softball an opportunity for international recognition and growth. And over the years, nations from different continents embraced softball and developed competitive teams. That led to many memorable moments for softball fans from around the world.

The 2004 Games were held in Athens, Greece. The US team won its third straight gold medal, and did so in dominant fashion. The Americans won their first eight games, all by shutout, thanks to a powerful pitching crew of Lisa Fernandez, Jennie Finch, and Cat Osterman. They finally surrendered a run in a 5–1 defeat of Australia in the gold-medal game. Known as the Real Dream Team, the 2004 US squad was inducted into the US Olympic & Paralympic Hall of Fame.

The first great Olympic upset came in 2008 in Beijing, China. Team USA was just as intimidating as in 2004, winning its seven pool-play games by a combined score of 53–1. The Americans defeated Japan 7–0 in that round and again 4–1 in the semifinals. But facing Japan a third time in the gold-medal match, the Americans finally stumbled. Pitcher Yukiko Ueno held the US batters to just five hits in a 3–1 shocker that gave Japan the gold medal.

That would be the last Olympic tournament for a while, as softball was not included in the 2012 Games, held in London, England, or the 2016 Games in Rio de Janeiro, Brazil. But with Tokyo, Japan, as the 2020 host, softball returned. Those Olympics were postponed to 2021. When they finally took place, the host country defended its gold medal with a 2–0 defeat of Team USA in the final.

Softball's presence in the Olympics has helped the sport gain popularity in regions where it was previously less recognized, including Europe, Africa, and Asia. Softball was removed from the slate of competitions for the 2024 Games in Paris, France. But it was added back to the Games for 2028.

Japanese players surround starting pitcher Yukiko Ueno (white glove), after she pitched a 2–0 shutout of the United States in the 2021 gold-medal game.

CHAPTER SIX

THE WORLD SERIES

A bead of sweat drips down the pitcher's face. The bases are loaded. The opposing bench is a hive of activity, cheering, chanting, and clapping. The crowd rises to its feet. The batter digs in. The pitcher winds and delivers.

It's the place where dreams come true and where legends are made. It's the WCWS, college softball's biggest stage. Every June, thousands of fans flock to Oklahoma City, Oklahoma, to watch eight of the nation's top teams fight for the national championship.

The first WCWS took place in 1969 in Omaha, Nebraska. College softball had a different governing body back then. In 1982, the National Collegiate Athletic Association (NCAA) took control of the sport. Since then, the WCWS has been the final part of the annual NCAA Women's Softball Tournament.

USA Hall of Fame Stadium in Oklahoma City always has an intense atmosphere for the WCWS.

Jennie Finch leaps off the mound to celebrate her 1–0 victory over UCLA in 2001.

Each season, 64 Division I softball teams from across the country compete in the NCAA Tournament. The tournament consists of three parts. In the first segment, 16 groups of four teams play a mini-tournament. This is the regional round.

The 16 winners of the regionals advance to the super regional round. The teams are seeded No. 1 through No. 16, with the highest seeds playing the lowest seeds. Each matchup is a best-of-three series. The first team to win two games advances. The eight winners of the super regional round advance to the WCWS. Those eight teams play until there are only two remaining. The finalists play a best-of-three series to determine the national champion.

USA Hall of Fame Stadium in Oklahoma City hosts all WCWS games. It has room for 13,000 fans. It's part of a complex that also holds the National Softball Hall of Fame and Museum, adding to the sense of history and tradition surrounding the event.

The tournament has created some unforgettable moments for fans and players alike. In 2001, Arizona pitcher Jennie Finch was on a roll. She finished the season 32–0 with a 0.54 earned run average (ERA). Finch capped her perfect season with a 1–0 shutout of the University of California, Los Angeles (UCLA) in the WCWS final.

Four years later, a surprise team pulled off a big upset. Schools from the South and West had dominated college softball up to that point. Michigan had won only two games in seven previous

TUNING IN

The WCWS has grown in popularity over the years, in large part due to ESPN and ABC broadcasting all of the games. In 2023, an average of 1.1 million fans tuned in to watch each WCWS game. And Oklahoma's victory over Florida State in the clinching game drew more than double that total.

WCWS appearances going into 2005. But the Wolverines got hot at the right time. They reached the championship, a best-of-three series against UCLA. The teams split the first two games and were tied 1–1 going into the 10th inning of the final game.

Two Michigan batters reached base. With two outs, freshman Samantha Findlay came to the plate. The first baseman had already hit 20 home runs on the season. And she'd driven in the Wolverines' only run of the night. Findlay hammered UCLA pitcher Anjelica Selden's 1–1 pitch over the left-field fence. Findlay pumped her fist as she circled the bases. Her teammates mobbed her at home plate. Then the Wolverines went out and got the final three outs to win 4–1 and take home their first national title.

Findlay's blast, and Michigan's win, has been credited with changing the game of softball. It gave hope to teams who weren't traditional powers that they might be able to win a title, too. "It was probably one of the greatest things for our sport, was to have somebody east of the Mississippi River win a national championship," Alabama coach Patrick Murphy said. "Especially a cold weather school, they had everything going against them, for sure. For them to do it, it paved the way for a lot."

Michigan players wait to celebrate with Samantha Findlay (16) after her national championship–clinching home run in 2005.

CHAPTER SEVEN

DYNASTIES

All sports have their share of powerful teams that tend to dominate the competition for years at a time. College softball is no exception. For years, the center of the college softball world was out west, specifically in two schools who took turns winning their conference title. Softball's NCAA era began in 1982. Arizona won its eighth national title in 2007. UCLA captured its 12th in 2019.

For a while, it seemed as if those were the only two teams with a chance at winning. Between 1988 and 1999, UCLA and Arizona combined to win 11 of the 12 WCWS championships. They met in the championship series five times in that span. UCLA's run was bolstered by numerous superstars. But there are none more important than Lisa Fernandez. The right-handed pitcher is considered by many to be the greatest softball player of all time. She was an ace on the mound and a slugger at the plate. In her senior year of 1993, Fernandez led the nation with a 0.25 ERA. At the same time, her .510 batting average was the best in the country.

The UCLA Bruins celebrate their NCAA-record 12th national championship after beating Oklahoma 5–4 in 2019.

Fernandez led the Bruins to two WCWS titles and two second-place finishes. She also spent several years as an assistant coach for the Bruins under Kelly Inouye-Perez. Together they led the Bruins to national titles in 1999, 2003, 2004, 2010, and 2019.

The late 1990s and early 2000s saw a new generation of Bruins stars. Stacey Nuveman's power hitting helped UCLA win the national title in 1999. The catcher ended her career in 2002 with a .466 batting average, the third-best in NCAA history. She's UCLA's all-time leader in home runs and runs batted in (RBIs).

While Nuveman succeeded with power, shortstop Natasha Watley was all about speed. The shortstop was a four-time first-team All-American at UCLA. Watley hit .450 in her career, and set Bruins records with 395 hits, 252 runs scored, and 158 stolen bases.

The Bruins won six of their titles between 1982 and 1990.

COMING ON STRONG

Oklahoma has emerged as the latest dynasty in college softball. The Sooners won three straight WCWS titles starting in 2021. That gave them six championships between 2013 and 2023. Their best team might have been the 2023 squad. They set an NCAA record by winning 53 straight games and finished the season with a 61–1 record, setting a new standard for college softball.

Then Arizona took its turn atop the college softball world. The Wildcats won their first national title in 1991. By 2001, they'd added five more WCWS championships to their trophy case. Back-to-back titles in 2006 and 2007 gave

Lisa Fernandez was the Pac-12 player of the year three times while at UCLA.

head coach Mike Candrea eight championships.

The list of outstanding Wildcats begins with Jennie Finch. In addition to her 32–0 season and Olympic gold medals, Finch was named the National Softball Player of the Year in 2001 and 2002. Meanwhile, outfielder Caitlin Lowe—who took over for Candrea as head coach in 2022—was a great player as well. Her .446 batting average is second-best in school history, and she holds the Wildcats career record for stolen bases.

LAURA ESPINOZA

Slugging shortstop Laura Espinoza helped put Arizona softball on the map. She hit 42 home runs combined between the 1993 and 1994 seasons, helping the Wildcats win national titles in each year. In 1995, Espinoza smashed pitches like no player before or since. She set NCAA records of 37 home runs and 137 runs batted in her senior season.

Caitlin Lowe, *left*, helped Arizona win the 2007 national championship as a player.

CHAPTER EIGHT

THE LONG BALL

Oklahoma was facing Central Florida in Game 1 of a three-game 2022 NCAA super regional. The team that won the series would advance to the WCWS. Oklahoma already led 3–0 in the bottom of the second when Jocelyn Alo stepped to the plate.

After falling behind in the count 2–0, the Central Florida pitcher knew she had to deliver a strike. She threw a fastball over the middle of the plate. And Alo was waiting for it.

With a flick of her wrists and a slight uppercut swing, Alo jumped all over the pitch. She blasted the ball high and deep to left-center field. Alo watched the arc of the ball as she trotted out of the batter's box. But she didn't see where it landed. Neither did anyone else. The ball had left the stadium. The ball cleared the outfield bleachers, a monster

In addition to setting the NCAA record for home runs while at Oklahoma, Jocelyn Alo also had a 40-game hitting streak spanning the 2020 and 2021 seasons.

NCAA CAREER HOME RUN LEADERS

Jocelyn Alo's 122 career home runs are 27 more than the next-highest total. Former Oklahoma star Lauren Chamberlain left the Sooners in 2015 with 95. In between, three other players came close to the record. Katiyana Mauga of Arizona hit 92 between 2014 and 2017. Arizona's Jessie Harper had that same total when she left school in 2021. Mississippi State's Mia Davidson also had 92 when she finished her college career in 2022.

shot that gave Oklahoma a 6–0 lead. It also put the Sooners well on their way to another trip to the WCWS.

The home run was nothing new to Alo, who burst onto the college scene as a freshman in 2018 with 30 homers. She led the nation with 34 home runs in 2021 and matched that total again the next year.

Alo made it look far too easy, to the point that even longtime Oklahoma coach Patty Gasso began to take her skills for granted. "When she comes up, I'm expecting her to hit a home run, probably like anybody else," Gasso said. "It's ridiculous that I'm thinking that way."

Coaches such as Gasso might think that notion is ridiculous because the home run hasn't always been a big part of fast-pitch softball. The sport had long been dominated by pitching. In fact, in the first 13 years of the NCAA era, the final score of the WCWS championship game

Alo hit her record-breaking 96th home run at a tournament in Hawaii, her home state.

was 1–0 or 2–0 eight times. But high-scoring games are much more common now. "Very seldom do you see the 1–0 game anymore. . . . It's a rarity versus a common one like in the old days," Auburn coach Clint Myers said in 2015.

Offensive totals have climbed in recent years, but none more than home runs. In 2014, NCAA teams set a record by averaging 0.68 home runs per team per game. The next year, that total jumped to 0.77. In 2023, 74 of 286 Division I teams averaged more than 0.77 home runs per game.

Even without Alo, who graduated in 2022, Oklahoma led the nation with 1.89 homers per game.

Three of the top four all-time home run hitters finished their college careers either in 2021 or 2022. And all of the top five began playing in 2012 or later. Teams today aren't playing more games. But modern softball players are bigger and stronger than ever.

Many coaches and players also say that hitters now watch more video of top pitchers. That way they can hone their swings based on that day's matchup. Regardless of the reason, it's a whole new ballgame. Or as former Tennessee slugger Taylor Koenig put it, "It's just a hitter's game now."

Kiki Milloy of Tennessee led the nation with 25 home runs during the 2023 season.

CHAPTER NINE

SMALL BALL

Power has become a major part of any softball team's offensive attack. But softball hitters can succeed in many ways. And there's still room in the game for what many call "small ball."

Some hitters like to drop the ball down for a bunt. Others are great at putting a good, solid swing on the ball and driving it to the outfield. A small group has mastered the art of slap hitting.

The slap hit is a special skill. It takes a lot of coordination and concentration. Slap hitters typically start in the left-handed batter's box. That puts them closer to first base. When the pitcher delivers, the slapper crosses her left foot over her right as she shuffles to the right. With another step, she brings the bat down and slaps the ball into the ground. The goal is to put the ball in play and use her speed to get on base. With the slap, a hitter is often a step or two out of the batter's box at the time when most hitters would be just starting to run to first base.

San Diego State's Bella Espinoza lays down a bunt during an NCAA Tournament game against Arizona State in 2022.

RECORD SETTERS

Nicole Barber of Georgia holds the NCAA career record with 257 stolen bases. She played for the Bulldogs from 2001 to 2004. The single-season record for stolen bases is 80, held by Michelle Ward of East Carolina. She needed just 61 games to set the mark in 1994.

Good slap hitters can make a big impact on the game. Because they're usually fast runners, they can use their speed as a weapon when running the bases. In softball, a runner has to wait until the ball is pitched before they can leave their base. But with just 60 feet between bases, it doesn't take long for a speedster to steal a base.

Nevada's Chelie Senini stole 50 bases in 50 games in 2023. At one point in her career, she was successful on 59 straight attempts. Her coach, Linda Garza, knows that Senini's skills are a huge benefit to her team. "She's incredibly fast, gets great jumps, understands how to gain speed, and she's super fast in those first 60 feet," Garza said. "Once you learn how to do it, it's pretty amazing. You just can't be thrown out." As for the role of speed in softball, Garza added, "It's a way to produce runs and put pressure on the defense sometimes when you're not offensively doing things. I don't like to play against a team that runs, so I realized I needed to be a team that ran as well."

Chelie Senini's 50 stolen bases during the 2023 season set a Mountain West conference record.

CHAPTER TEN

THE PROFESSIONAL GAME

Professional softball in its early years was marked by exhibition games and barnstorming tours. During the mid-20th century, women's softball gained attention as a source of entertainment. Pro teams traveled across the United States to showcase their skills. They often drew big crowds and helped increase the popularity of the sport.

The first significant steps toward organized professional softball occurred in the 1970s and 1980s. The International Women's Professional Softball Association (IWPSA) was founded in 1976. It was the first professional league for women's softball players. The IWPSA featured 10 teams in cities throughout the country. Salaries ranged from $1,000 to

Many top players signed on with Athletes Unlimited when the league was formed in 2020.

Sammy Marshall, *right*, of the Chicago Bandits of National Pro Fastpitch slides in safely against Chinese team Beijing Shougang Eagles during a game in 2017.

$5,000 per year. The league lasted four seasons before folding due to financial trouble.

Fan interest in softball dropped during the 1980s. But the successes of the WCWS and the US women's national team helped create new opportunities for players. In 1997, the Women's Pro Softball League (WPSL) was founded. It later evolved into National Pro Fastpitch (NPF). NPF had its 2020 and 2021 seasons canceled because of COVID-19. The league officially suspended operations at that point.

Since then, Athletes Unlimited has become the top option for professional softball in the United States. Athletes Unlimited is a different type of league. The players are part owners of the organization. They share in the league's profits. The league plays for five weeks each year in Rosemont, Illinois. Each week, players are redrafted to new teams. No team wins the league. Individual players earn points for their season performance.

MILLION-DOLLAR ARM

In 2016, pitcher Monica Abbott signed a groundbreaking contract with the Houston-based Scrap Yard Dawgs in the NPF. The six-year deal was worth $1 million. It's believed that at the time it was the most money paid to any female team sports athlete in the United States.

Athletes Unlimited crowns one individual champion each season. Past winners have been Cat Osterman (2020), Aleshia Ocasio (2021), Dejah Mulipola (2022), and Odicci Alexander (2023).

Women's Professional Fastpitch launched as a more traditional league in 2023. One of the teams included was the USSSA Pride, which formerly played in NPF. The team also spent two years playing independently. They, like many softball fans, hope the new league will be a permanent home.

CHAPTER ELEVEN

SOFTBALL LEGENDS

In 1961, softball pitcher Joan Joyce faced off against baseball legend Ted Williams in a charity event. In front of 17,000 fans, Joyce fired several pitches past one of the greatest hitters in baseball history. It was just one of many feats in Joyce's career. Playing at a time when not many people knew about women's fast-pitch softball, Joyce won more than 750 games while playing for amateur teams. She also threw an estimated 50 perfect games.

As soon as softball emerged as a varsity college sport in the 1980s, the first wave of stars emerged. UCLA shortstop Dot Richardson led the pack. She led the Bruins to their first national title in 1982. And Richardson was still going strong in 1996. Facing China in the Olympic gold-medal game, Richardson came up with a runner on in the bottom of the third. She belted a two-run home run that proved the difference in a 3–1 win.

Richardson helped the United States repeat as gold medalists in 2000. But she wasn't the only legend on both teams. Right-handed pitcher Lisa Fernandez pitched for three Olympic teams between 1996

Dot Richardson celebrates crossing the plate during a game against Puerto Rico at the 1996 Olympics.

and 2004. In 74 2/3 innings, she allowed only four earned runs. Fernandez also struck out 21 batters in one game in 2000 to set an Olympic record. She was also a great hitter. At the 2004 Games, Fernandez hit a record .545.

Fernandez teamed up with two other superstar pitchers at the 2004 games. Righty Jennie Finch and lefty Cat Osterman joined Fernandez in allowing only one run throughout the entire tournament. In 2008, *Time* magazine named Finch the most famous softball player in the world. Meanwhile, Osterman was just beginning a long career. She pitched in the gold-medal game for the United States in 2021. She also was the winning athlete in the first Athletes Unlimited softball season.

Opposing Osterman in the gold-medal game in 2021 was Japan's Yukiko Ueno. The then 39-year-old righty was already a legend. In the 2004 Olympics, she became the first pitcher to throw a perfect game

HITTING LEGENDS

There have been many great hitters throughout softball history. Alison McCutcheon of Arizona set an NCAA record with 405 career hits. Catcher Crystl Bustos of Team USA was one of the game's great power hitters. She hit 13 career home runs in three Olympic Games. That includes a record of six at the 2008 tournament in Beijing.

in the tournament. Ueno capped her legendary career by outdueling Osterman and giving Japan its second Olympic gold.

Yukiko Ueno's fastball has reached 80 miles per hour (128 km/h). She is considered the hardest thrower in the sport.

GLOSSARY

alloy

A strong material made by combining one or more metal elements.

amateur

A person who plays a sport without getting paid.

arc

A curved path, often made by something traveling through the air.

barnstorming

Traveling to perform shows or play games.

composite

Something that is made from various parts.

dynasty

A team that has an extended period of success, usually winning multiple championships in the process.

exhibition

A game that doesn't count in the standings.

fair territory

The area between the first-base line and the third-base line on a baseball or softball field, where the ball is live if it lands.

perfect game

A complete game in which a team retires every opposing batter and allows no base runners.

recreational

Describing an activity done for fun.

reflexes

Actions that are performed without thinking.

rivalry

Two opponents that have a fierce and ongoing competition.

tactics

Strategies.

MORE INFORMATION

Books

Abbott, Monica, with Debby and Rob Schriver. *Rise and Shine: The Monica Abbott Story*. University of Tennessee, 2023.

Flynn, Brendan. *Girls' Softball*. Abdo, 2022.

Stathes, Corbu. *Everything Baseball*. Abdo, 2025.

Online Resources

To learn more about softball, please visit **abdobooklinks.com** or scan this QR code. These links are routinely monitored and updated to provide the most current information available.

INDEX

About the Author

Sean Shapiro is a freelance author and journalist living in Michigan. He and his wife, Christina, are the proud parents of Evangeline and Dean.